CW01660277

Painting t

Poems by

BIBHU PADHI

Sangam Books

SANGAM BOOKS LIMITED
57 London Fruit Exchange
Brushfield Street
London E1 6EP, U.K.

By arrangement with
Orient Longman Limited
3-6-272 Himayatnagar
Hyderabad 500 029 (A.P.), India

Published by
Sangam Books Limited 1999

ISBN 0 86311 796 1

Typeset by
OSDATA, Hyderabad 500 029

Printed in India at
M/s Ram Graphics, Mumbai 400 022

Bibhu Padhi (b. 1951) has published his poems in distinguished magazines and periodicals throughout the English-speaking world, such as *Contemporary Review, Encounter, The Poetry Review, The New Criterion, Poetry, TriQuarterly,* and *Kavya Bharati*. He has also written a book-length study of D. H. Lawrence and, with his wife, Minakshi Padhi, a reference book on Indian Philosophy and Religion. At present, he is completing a series of poems, tentatively called *Meditations on Being*, each of which is based on a single Upanishadic *sloka*. He lives at Puri-on-Sea, where he teaches English at SCS College. *Painting the House* is his fourth book of poems.

Other poetry collections in this series

A Harvest of Light SUMA JOSSON
A Spelling Guide to Woman CHARMAYNE D'SOUZA
Fire, Water, Earth and Wind P. S. REGE
Indian English Poetry since 1950: an Anthology ed. VILAS SARANG
Looking Back SANJIV BHATLA
No Entry for the New Sun: Translations from Modern Marathi Dalit Poetry ed. ARJUN DANGLE
Time's Crossroads ROBIN NGANGOM
Woolgathering SHIV K. KUMAR

Acknowledgements

The author is grateful to the editors of the following magazines in which some of these poems first appeared:

"House Lizards" in *Encounter* (London, England)
"Midnight Consolings" in *Poetry* (Chicago; copyright, 1989, Modern Poetry Society.)
"Annual Invitation to the Dead," "Home", and "Ceasework" in *Tri-Quarterly* (Copyright, 1988 & 1989, Northwestern University)
"Crossing Over" in *Poetry Wales* (England)
"Something Else" in *The Poetry Review* (London)

"Something Else" is reprinted in *Remembering Ray: A Composite Biography of Raymond Carver*, eds. William Stull and Maureen Carroll (Santa Barbara: Capra Press, 1993).

For their encouragement, the author is indebted to James Merrill, Tess Gallagher, Naomi Shihab Nye, Robert Richman, Richard Wilbur, Nissim Ezekiel, and the late William Stafford.

To the Memories of

Anantaram Rath
Madan Mohan Rath
Digambara Rath
Bhavagrahi Mishra
and
Narayan Pati

grandparents

Contents

The Bed

With a smell of yesterday, the day before,
of the past. Of now, of today, this minute.
Of what remains stretched all along the sheet
below the lean figure that sleeps.
A thickness of accumulation, of what
the body gives over to every small bit
of a thing it longs to touch. Of what it
receives — things offered away
long back, in sleep, including those
inimitable dreams. The unwarily gathered-up
dust of the skin, its darker premises
loosening while the long night waits.

Every turn in sleep folds into
the inert raw lines of a deep deep black.
A friendship built through sweat and dreams,
a stickiness of familiarity. And a willingness
to let all of these stay as they are,
untampered with, through years
of a humiliation that the bed alone knows
regardless of your common everyday wish
to change the sheets.

Watching on a Summer Afternoon Children Playing

Fine creatures of the afternoon
sun, which is still strong enough
to last a lifetime of play and shout.
The loose, raw dust of summer
is in their eyes; they don't care.
Their bodies rolling on the bare earth,
tumbling each other over, crawling with
innumerable hands and feet, each entwined
with the others, like a group of crabs that is
unable to move elsewhere, far from here,
for fear of losing the close, familiar touch.

Shadows rise over the grassless soil,
hover and dance above the fringes
of their skin, pierced now by
the outgoing sun, shining through
a deep refraction of small voices.
They seem to be far from here, where
I sit watching the modest dreams take shape
in the distance that separates us.

My usual late-afternoon sleep
refused to take me in a long time ago;
and now the yes-clouds are gathering

on what was once a clear, cloudless sky.
The streets look empty, barren almost,
the town is without any other sound,
as if disowning everything except
these small children playing in the dust.

The first drops of rain begin to fall.
I guess it's the first pre-monsoon shower
of the year. Dreams of green fields
return from the northern valleys,
from just under the Himalayas.
Which other dream, harder
to achieve than the present ones,
might lurk above the dirty, sun-baked bodies
of children, now playing in the rain?

Poem for My Son

1.

I seem to know all about you:
your time, your place, your name,
the clean Indian-wheat colour
of your skin, your unpolished words.

But I know that there're also sounds
that you do not know, shapes
that you wouldn't recognize.
For instance, the owl's lean dark
cry, or the sea at Puri
during a small moon's night.

And, at this hour, when
you are breathing so quietly
beside your mother,
I seem to hear a faraway whisper
that almost tells me
you're not mine.

I hear the owl's late cry,
the gentle expanding roar
of the blue waters of Puri.
Never mind. I know where my night
sleeps, undisturbed by every
sound and thought, so peacefully.

2.

I know very little about you.
Since the hour of your arrival,
I've been too busy with
devious sleep and ways of
earning it, to be with you.

I count the minutes during
our play and laughter,
stagnate within the curse of my
longing to be free.

Your tiny hands hold my fingers
and lead me to your kingdom
of challenge and shout —
a place where small feet have
just begun to walk upon new ground.

Why do you smile so remotely?
Could it be that I've neglected
my own rights to be with you?
For, even when I throw the rubber ball
at the wall and persuade you
to bring it back to me, I know
there're still other games
we could play willingly —
those that the bodies alone
participate in, without
the interference of the mind,
your clean naked skin shining in a pure dance
of togetherness above mine.

Although, just now I'm afraid
to continue even this simple game
of our bodies belonging to
another place and time
through a sheer exchange of smiles.

In the Temple

I came here to pray.
At the short entrance, guarded by
alert lions on a pedestal of fame,
people touch the wall, stand erect,
murmur blessings to themselves.

A smell of burnt wicks fills
the marbled courtyard.
The goddess's face can hardly be seen
behind the veil of smoke
and loud singing and raised hands.

The polished floors, slippery
and deceitful, wouldn't hold my feet.
Does the goddess know that
I could hardly stand upright
in her archaic territory?

What if it is only a test
of my willingness to accept defeat?
Although I've decided to stand
here, my words drifting sluggishly
in the stagnant air, until they reach

her threshold of innocence and familiarity.

Diwali

The evening is alive on all our
coloured faces. Green, blue, an intermittent
red, a whiteness of blinding rage.

The sounds of the heavens exploding
could be heard among the loud shouts
of children dancing on the streets.

Despite your wish not to be there,
you are already here, among colours
and sounds, without your knowledge,

sharing in the cracks that open in the newmoon sky,
in between stars, in those dark regions
showing through the slits of your wishes.

You could be here, there, anywhere,
but the sounds and colours won't let you escape,
the lights will find you out from the dark at last.

Except where a new birth is taking its earthwise shape
in another darkness, in the long shadow of a dream,
in the clear, first notes of a defenceless cry.

Soft, irregular, shadowy as consolation.
Coming as an answer to the lights and sounds
that you may not believe to be near and true.

The cry of a lifetime, as if it knew
our commonplace mistakes of identity,
our confusing arrivals with departures.

Somewhere else, someone, who knew all about us
and shared with us all these colours and sounds
over the years, is going to escape

through the cracks of our own making
to another land, to accomplish our
dreams of inheriting the beyonding places.

You can see him astride the many-coloured rocket
that your child let go, rushing towards the stars
in an all-knowing trajectory of arched motion.

Sleep

Locating our own sleep is another matter.
Now, when sleep is so wide awake
over comfortable beds and floors,
so complete over the platforms of withdrawal.

This my child doesn't know, wouldn't care for,
now that he jumps and runs about his forgetful dance
of nakedness, throwing off the near limits of time
and space, accommodating other dimensions of our race.

What if all the dates were consequent upon
one another, each closely enclosed by others
in an embrace of effective love, pure reason?
That's so, and so are my child's disregarding ways.

Has he been too far into sleep now to note our sleep's
necessary course, its promise of reawakened love?
Or how that sleep can harass our common wish
to find ourselves every day, differently, when ignored?

It's we who feel troubled anyway
and thus find ourselves differently placed —
far outside his easy, ever-awakened love
which so undisturbedly takes care of itself.

And so we seek our proper sleep elsewhere,
beyond the closely linked nights and days, while
he continues to dance in his exotic outfit of smiles,
plays on us his shrewd tricks of wakefulness.

Of Hiding Important Things

For William Stafford

The world wouldn't take them with
a smile. I know. Or, if it did,
it'd show them up every time
you began to speak of humbler things.
It'd tell you that they weren't things
that one ever gave to another
or even kept to oneself during
the worst of times. Things
that arrived without purpose, in between
modes of usual, commonplace business
and disturbed the ways of give and take.
You may not blame the world for this.
It never gave them to you on its own
and hence, is not bound to take them back.

The best thing, therefore, is to keep them
to yourself, lay them under such nights
that even time forgets, let them breathe
the soft lunar air, acquire the darkness
that is elsewhere, looking for such things.
And then, ask your grandchild
to gather them up for you —
delicate fingers feeling the distance
of their shape and size, before
handing them over to you, in the hope that
these things which their innocence

longed to touch for a long time,
are indeed placed in safe hands, waiting
to be laid back again, touched, gathered,
and given back to you, preserved for a future time.

Today

Is the question to all the days
that have gone before, shall come.

The question that lies quietly above
the perfect upper half of the first sun,

pretending sleep, taking over
the sun's mellow orange colour.

That rises with the rising sun,
hurting my eyes, teasing my migraine.

That stands upright above my shoulders,
numbing my every limb with the burden

of questions of all my yesterdays.
That quietly travels west, ripens,

becomes the evening air that arrives late.
That only seems to disappear with

the outgoing sun, while it spreads
all over earth and sky.

Is the answer to all the endured days
and those that wait to come.

The uninvited answer of dreams
inside my intermittent sleep —

the one that I never framed
nor shall ever know how it came.

Midnight Consolings

These are different in tone and theme
from the ones that we prepare
so discreetly during the day.
More from the heart, from
that corner where it keeps its
dark promises secure from our
habitual wishes. The cry
that wakes from sleep couldn't be
left alone so easily.
At a different time, it would've
found its end, perhaps in a game
of words or a play of eyes.
But now, in the dark, it is
different. Louder, less precise,
asking for nothing.
Our voices soften at these times,
as if they had learnt something
from the night —
its slow meditative course over
houses and streets, its pure spontaneity.
The residual dreams hover before
our invisible eyes, urging us
to pause and listen
to the reasonless cry, now diffusing
into our nights. Our bodies

are half-dreaming still, while
our generous words issue from
a place far within this night.

House Lizards

In these tropical homes, they are many,
but they keep mostly to themselves and eat only
those insects who gratefully offer themselves.

They are believed to be right, always.
When we differ on a critical point, from behind
the piles of old newspapers will come the words:

True, true.

During a crisis in thought, when everything large
and small is bound into a knot that
won't open despite our best efforts;

or when, at the lean lost end
of an imagining hour, we find ourselves
farther than we were, we hear:

True, true.

Reptilian group. Cream-white and smoke-grey.
Harmless. Preservers of ancient memories.
Our wise forefathers in enviable disguise.

The First Painting

For Buddhaditya

The handmade sheet of paper
sits below a set of small, anxious fingers.
The sound of the night descending
could be heard on the neighbouring terraces,
away among the deodars near College Square —
throaty voices of children withdrawing
into their mothers' loud calling,
the chirping of gathering birds
among tall leaves and branches.

There should be ways of defining
things other than the nearer ones;
of colouring the secret, spare places
of the mind. The minutes move.
On the floor, the off-white sheet of paper
lies flat and mute. The one-inch wide brush
is dipped into a cupful of unwilling water —
once, twice, and then is left there.

Several minutes later, when the brush
is used at last, it is only to wash
the paper's face, to take its blank look off.
A spot of vermilion-red appears
at the still centre, and then spreads
until it reaches its farthest limits.
The thick brush moves again

on the remaining space. The mark spreads,
the first sun begins to shine on his face
while his eyes shine back, even though
the edges are blurred and blurring still.
My humble world begins and ends at this place.

A Face in the Dark

For Siladitya

"Watch me, watch me carefully," it whispered,
"and you'll find the differences you never expected."
I had thought that what I saw was God's
finest achievement since Creation —
flawless, perfect in every nook
and corner, and yet human beyond doubt.
It was the pair of tiny eyes gazing
into my eyes gazing in wonder at what
could've been my child's apparent face —
the eyes sure of what they saw despite
our self-contradictions, worries of the night.

"Watch carefully." I took my beating time —
the long eyes shining somewhere between
dream and sleep, the lips closed tight, as if
challenging my power of reasonable speech.
"I don't see anything misplaced, wrong," I whispered
back. "Everything looks so proper, so
finely wrought by a hand that knew
what it did or was going to, a hand that knew its business."
The hands, the fingers, the feet, the toes.
"Watch again," it whispered. "Don't you see
how the inner corner of the left eye
should've been less acute than it is now,
just a degree or two less than the right?"
Perhaps. Perhaps, yes. Yes, indeed yes;
the voice was vehemently right, it was so.

"Watch carefully." The old words took shape
again. "Don't you think the skin should've been
lighter, a feather in the wind, so you could
touch it while you never really did, felt its
texture in your blood only, the way your blood
flowed in your veins, without your help
or knowledge, in the darkness of sleep?"
Yes. Yes, maybe yes. Perhaps I thought so.
I could feel the blood getting warmer
as during seasons of success and insult,
my eyes beginning to see clearer
the things I thought were
always mine but were never so.
The stars feel all through the long night,
the slight moon became slighter, the clouds appeared.
I could feel the smile that came from
far away, from beyond the expanse of time and hope,
and lodged exactly where the eyes flawed.

"Watch again." The voice was peremptory,
familiar, and clear, like my own
righteous hands that could do no wrong,
their too efficient fingers. "Don't you think
the smile should've been thinner, its course
a little more unfamiliar, its shocks and surprises
just a little more devious than your knowledge
of its purpose and promise, its ancient source
gentle as a god's look, an angel's mercy,
generous like the first God's benediction?"
Yes, it could've been that too;
it wasn't unkind, that much I knew.

But then, perhaps yes. Yes. Yes, perhaps.
But no. No. The slanted eyes of the later-rising sun
told me so and also my six-month-old son's clean

undisturbed face of sleep. Who else was there?
What happened in the night that was so terrible
that I now begin to doubt it ever did?
The voiceless words hung about me still:
"Watch me carefully ... watch me now."

In This City of Merchants

You are the exiled one.
No one listens to your words.
And you walk through its lanes —
silent, thinking, looking for someone
who might be looking for you.
But the windows are shut and sealed,
the doors locked. Why should they
look for you, you only?
Buying and selling are too absorbing
an occupation to take notice of you.

When you wrote the last line
of the poem that broke your frail sleep,
you alone knew that what your
lean hands held so affectionately
couldn't wake others from
their long trade with sleep and dream.
You read out your lines, the air trembles.
And then, at the end of it all,
the long, cryptic silence of your
own words madly rushing back at you.

A Man of our Time

For William Golding

You are like some figure in marble
that I've longed to see, perhaps touch
when no one is looking. Archaic,
freckled with spots of ancient time.
You sit among familiar faces, distant
as a hard-working longshoreman
in a company of city-dwellers.
Inscribing your name on the title page
of a copy of *The Scorpion God* that I
place before you, you look up and smile;
the moment seems too close to bear.
In the lecture hall, you read
from what might've been your own story.
Your voice belongs somewhere else,
far from the Cornwall where William was born —
a place too far within Earth's history
for any one of us to be in.
You confess, you've been reading a book
that dates back to a year
that hasn't changed until this day
and will not nine hundred years from now.
Will this go on forever, beyond
all ends and conclusions? If it is so,
let it be so, for in the dark future
of mankind's dubious, diabolic course,
someone somewhere would wait for you

to emerge from the haze of history
and quietly listen to what you say.
A story of our time, our place.

Wintering Guests

It has been winter all through the year.
Winter, numbness, winter.
The arctic chill quietly issues from
heart, mind, lips, hands and feet,
but from the mind, especially.
The seasons have been waiting
to let themselves in and flower,
but they have kept themselves out
ever since they arrived here,
following time's usual course.
Their words hold us in a typical gesture
of compassion, while meanings
spread over us enormously, like snow in the north.
We merely hope and wait, for we lost our
own words one summer evening amid
the changelessness of a severe chill.
What kind of human warmth can open
these doors, now sealed by a cold self-sufficiency?
We move slow, among our children who know
very little about the exact nature
of each season and its consequences.
And when we are somewhat alone, we try to trace
the cause of our freezing limbs and speech
and watch the mist issuing in circles
from above their statuesque heads.

A Sense of Place

The place we look for is not
the place we should be travelling to.

The place that we know as our own
isn't the one that has stayed with us.

The place we've been led to
isn't one that we might call our own.

The sun shines otherwise than
in geography, the air smells old;

the light moves slow, is slight, falling
at the place where the heart is believed to be.

We wait, but nothing shows that might've recalled
in a clear way a breath lost among night and time

not long ago.
A place

of our own, a dream of living
fulfilled by all our dreams of acting.

What hope is still alive that might
carry us towards the desired place?

A familiar name, a fond act of remembering,
a place we might know and recognise?

The place we've been led to by blind hands
couldn't be one that we might call our own.

The place we look for is not the place
we should be travelling to.

Annual Invitation to the Dead

We call them over every year
on the new-moon day following *Siva Rātri* —
my father, and his, and his,
and their companions in peace.
February is somewhere between
last winter and the harsh Indian summer.

Sitting on the floor, in front of
a square figure drawn with rice flour,
and repeating the chants the priest recites,
I lean towards the past, which
now seems farther than ever.

My ancestors —
inhabitants of thin layers
of miraculous air, our well-wishers
during hours of pain and pleasure —
are once more here, unseen and yet
participating in the earth's rites.
I've inherited their responsibilities
towards the innumerable dead.

They arrive and depart, annually,
to confirm that I'm still here,
with my wife and my child, true
in every earthly way, like the wind

through the trees, and with a memory
that's alive still and may not ignore
their far, only too distant company.

Portrait of a Family

The handsome woman who is lying straight
on her bed, is listening to the ticking seconds —
her head now resting on a raised platform
of pillows, her soft wheat-coloured body
now covered with dark sores, her eyes
half-looking and half-amazed
at things that once were hers.
In the air, heavy with November,
there's a sense of waiting.
Her children are eager to see her lips move
for the last time and speak a word that'll stay.
Her married daughters (now "living happily ever after"),
need her story come to a quiet close, for
much of its shock is gone and nearly over.
Her only son, a mere boy of nineteen,
is ready to perform
any stupid act
that might be waylaid by his helplessness.

The man who is crouching near her feet,
is supposed to have been teaching others how animals
live and function, how the frogs collect their
ignorant food and the cells divide and grow
what we see, feel and hear.
He is now weeping in the adjacent room, in silence,
once in a while coming in, passing his hands over

her cheeks, her forehead and lips,
over her fingers that look delicate still,
even now, the soles of her feet that are
still warm from the new, nameless fever of loneliness.
It seems he is finding her for the first time
in thirty-three years, during which he might've known
women of all colours, wishes and kinds.

This last, long night of waiting is
what he has never passed through before.
As I walk out of the room for the last time,
I see him holding her naked feet, leaning
after them despite his own history of backache.

All this was two nights ago
and I haven't tried to know if
she is still lying straight on her bed
with her children and her man
around her, counting the seconds as they
drift by, ignorant of every single grief.
I think I've known all this far too long
not to care for what might've happened
that night for the first and final time.
As I write this, I can almost hear a line
travel back through the early sun and bird-cries:
"You built this home and I only wish
you had lived a little longer to see
how, after you, it broke and crumbled —
in spite of me, in spite of me."

Paper Town

Cuttack was being re-enacted by delicate hands.
Long rows of newspapered roads joined each other
and left blank spaces where, among other things,
the new Municipal Market, Gobind Sahu's grocery store,
the town's vast stadium, the ancient fort
of Barabati, and our house, were securely placed.
My son and his enthusiastic friends, all familiar
with the town in more than just a geographical way,
tried to explain every turn or twist of a road,
each dark corner where delicacies were being served
until late evenings, every blind lane and alley
through which no one walked for the simple fear of ghosts.
"We know more about Cuttack than you or any one
of your mad friends do," my six-year son proudly claimed.

That day, just about when the evening rain
was about to commence its routine spray,
a fierce wind tore past doors and windows,
striking down every little thing on its way.
Somewhere, a loud humming of a storm; the house trembled.
While I sat outside, on the half-circular balcony,
waiting for a different rain, my son
rushed out with a fretted laughter on his face.
Finding his place on my lap, his small face
drawn secretly close to mine, he whispered:
"That stupid wind has taken away large chunks

of our town. It lifted Uncle B's house
seven feet above the ground before crashing it down.
You know, our house was about to go, but I
held on to it with all my hands and limbs."
And then, bursting with a thunderous laughter,
he announced in a self-declaring way:
"You know, Nana, Gobind Sahu's rootless shop
is lying helplessly on the large bed of the Mahānadi ...
You don't believe me? You'd better go and find it
for yourself." [He was laughing louder than
the thunder now]. "Poor fellow ... his things
are all mixed up now: sugar with tablets
of 'Crowning Glory', the coarse sand-mixed rice
with Johnson's supremely soft 'Baby Lotion'.
Let's go for once and see what the wind has done."
I went in; he was right, perfectly so.
His good friends were trying desperately
to retrieve the town from a terrible mess
that could only take care of itself. Tomorrow.

Ceasework

Since it began, the perspectives
haven't changed much. The classrooms,
quiet as ever, but now empty
of their blank faces, show themselves
as ideal models of the past.

The blackboards are darker
than yesterday, the floors
strewn with betel juice, pieces
of writing chalk, torn leaflets.

A fear of the present stalks
the corridors roughened by
intending feet, tempting us
to shout with larger voices.
But what, in any case,
could our words do except claim
the mythic peace in the future?

Elsewhere, I imagine, the ministers
are discussing the newest ways
of raising public taxes, the need
of the currency changing hands,
among whispers. Their words define
our needs calculatedly, against
the heavy backdrop of industrial
development, welfare of the poor.

The poor have remained so
since the time our grandfathers
dreamt of their homes, land, and wives.
I've refused to own any dreams now,

having gifted all those dreams away
to children with distended stomachs
listening to speeches on integration
and unity, the country's rich culture.

Today I can only hope to see
how it feels to be there, among
the lonely blackboards
and naked children playing
in the rain, despite
well-written speeches,
unspoken hunger.

"Ceasework" is a contemporary Indian word for "to go on strike."

This Green Light

This green light seems to be
everywhere, even at those places
where we had secretly buried
our nascent hopes, pale miseries.
The books, the white-and-blue tables
on which our children completed their
weekend homework without complaint,
the bed on which every night
we bundle into a frozen sleep,
the very blocks of moulded plastic
with which our younger, six-year old son
struggles to build his frail
formless worlds of innocence and simplicity —
every little thing seems to have been
transformed by this light into
the lucidity of April, joy and dreams.
This green light, which has been
so near our over-protected
shadows and sicknesses,
childlike hopes, adult miseries.

Kites

They belong to the sky.
In late winter, just about when
the first spring breeze
moves into the town,
errant children gather on rooftops
and laughingly let them go.
We wait, but this they know.

They rise gracefully, in lines
and circles, before hanging on
for a while, nodding
at one another like knowing birds.
As we watch them from here,
they fly into one another
and start performing a curling
and searching dance, leaning away
from a centre of blank space
that widens as their dance
gathers motion and love.
And then, one of them
suddenly lets itself go while
the others stare in dumb wonder.
The whole thing starts all over again,
as though to come together were
the only way to leave each other.
Hours later, the sky is clear

except for the high clouds,
the sun (lowering now),
and the memory of kites on a sky.

They've all gone in their
countless separate ways.
We wait for another season
of love and remembrance, when
they will reappear from nowhere
only to let themselves go once more.
We feel sorry, but *they know*.

Two Paintings by D.H. Lawrence

For Keith Sagar

1: "Boccaccio Story"

It's just this we've been waiting for —
an efficient hand's quiet, confident touch
on the deep-furrowed earth and heat,
the dogs' four-legged curiosity,
the nuns' ancient wish to witness how
life is born and renewed.

The trees in the distance watch intently
the drama of passion and insult.
The limp dark phallus is all its own
and seems to rise above the naked lines
of the figure that lies stretched out on his field,
exposed to the declining sun and the breeze.

I think of my late afternoon sleep
that should be full with allusive dreams.
Lorenzo: Before you're forced to leave us
once again for your fretful textual sleep,
let me just know if your careful gardener
now pretending sleep, is dreaming too!

2: "Dance Sketch"

Each small thing is part of the sun
and the wind. The lean trees

bend into one another in an act
of love that excludes magic and time.
The light explains the couple's
fluent rhythm of dance,
the leaning wind their
close intimacy. The goat knows all.

Do trees ever combine in this
too human way, each anxious
to touch the other in an embrace
that is unlikely to stay?
perhaps during the nights only,
avoiding our eyes of envy which
merely know how to imitate, when even
the sneaking moon stays out of the sky.

Maybe the brush was held light,
hovering almost, over the canvas
so it might descend with heaven's own colours —
gold-yellow, shimmering white.
But then, it is midday now
and the sun and the wind
are there, somewhere, out of it all
and yet, have given us this scene,
which is wild about its own splendour
in a child's self-forgetful way.

Among the Ruins

For Shabana Azmi

What else is left here except these?
The darkness encloses every stone
and leaf, corrupts the power of speech.
The sun, shadowed by forest leaves
and clouds of lonely and seeking eyes,
rarely appears, and no one knows.

There've been times when a nowhere voice
strayed into these ruins and soon discovered
that it couldn't belong to these nameless stones.
Bodies lie here, just a few of them that never knew
that there might be a way to escape the death
that has been so vastly alive far within themselves.

From within the dark, someone calls
someone who has been there, always;
a woman's face grown thin with waiting
looks at you, almost imploring you
to teach it how a smile could be made
or a lost name restored to its place.

The forest wind sweeps through
one of its innumerable alleys
where shadows of older times
are believed to stay, uncomplainingly.
What else is left here, except lips that

cannot move, eyes that cannot smile?
Proud, forbidding shadows that play among
the last of the pillars, arches, family albums,
doors and windows that never open?
No one knows; no one need know.

Konarak

I touch the stone's cold, move
my lean fingers over its surface;
I'm received by its quiet outwardness.
Somewhere, in the gathering dark,
a smile is known, and soon forgotten.

And then a whisper, a rush
of seawind over the stark sand
that holds the weight of centuries,
the thought of a distant sacrifice.

I walk past the naked body and feet,
past gestures of love and renewal,
the long-awaited anguish of fulfilment.
I bury in the sand the sound
of my mortal feet. The hard stones
begin to thaw and spread even as I hear
the unheard, slow dance of other feet.

Deep within the thawing stones
a child's lisping voice, banished
by our memory and the irreverent past.
How does one remember things?
Who shall hear my words, except
the silences deep within stones?
From these chance meetings, what
reward, what lost glory drifts in the air?

The Burnt Town

The town is filled with wounds
from burns that a fire of the past
inflicted on it years ago;
the stench of spoilt skin
travels through lanes that are
full of people who have chosen
to remain busy with healthier things —
one's very own wishes that find their ends
faithfully, despite our sleeplessness;
a mockery of the past that
even the past takes little notice of.
A vain ray of hope, soothing
in its own too delicate, tentative way,
moves with the early spring wind
towards the rooms where
thirsty, drugged bodies lie, waiting
for oxygenated air and time.

Songs of heroes could be heard
over the radio, the television celebrates
the country's fortieth anniversary
of independence from alien hands.
What have we been waiting for since then?
For which familiar touch, which
other way of surrender?
Which other way of surrender

to sweetness and health
can restore us to ourselves, without
the interference of the ever-eager
ministers of faith?
My own temperate nerves have started
giving way to the fire's dubious commands.
I fail to talk fluently about what happened
between health and this waiting for
the body's countless failures.

We know, the town shall remain
what it has been despite
well-recited sermons, prayers
for the dead and the dying —
a place where we have found ourselves
(helpless, praying) as if for the last time.
Work selflessly, without
any expectation of reward:
the cliche continues to haunt us
in our dreams while the burn-wounds
spread over the town's shrivelling skin,
taking over whatever little remained
clean and untouched till now.

Painting the House

You must know that it requires
a very different kind of dreaming
than any that you've known in the past.
The sort that is cautious about
the years that took care
of a variety of colours, as well as
the years ahead that might choose
to lie on the walls, without pondering ever
that it is the colours alone
that keep the house alive, sprightly.
The dream of the little-known birds
on the widespread terraces in the midst of
the harsh Indian Summer, of their
feathers strewing the once-clean floors
before they are carefully picked up
by your sixteen-month-old child, only to be
stuck on the blank walls by tentative fingers.
The long dream of elaborately carved cobwebs
that could simply be left where they are,
untouched, and also of the pigeon-warmth
of the tall sky-lit nests.
The dream of a line in blue chalk
that your child, now grown into a boy who
doesn't need your parental help anymore,
drew under the routine pressure
of your proud, tutoring fingers.

The dream of the maps of countries
you might not think much of,
of the school time-tables
of five consecutive years;
of the spot where your child stood
for three long hours four years ago
facing the wall, his tiny hands taking
the tears to the all too absorbent wall
while you sat on the chair, counting
the slow minutes of a punishment
that came without reason or thought.
The dream of the places where
the paint has come off the ceiling
to show the stains of last year's rain
at a time when, elsewhere, people walked
a long time to feel the endearing touch
of water on broken-dry skins.
All these and more. The ancient dream
that is shy to arrive, afraid of a past
that could be too far away to be
recognised and owned. The fear
of the years waiting to come,
the failures and hopes of a lifetime
buried deep in the smell
of the newly bought paint.

Neglected Absences

The burden of things is increasing
until, one day, these sinking hands
will fail to carry them through time.
The pressures of size and shape
the dumb exactness of weight
in a world in which things rule
over the fugitive departures of the mind.

The lizard on the wall behind me,
alert as ever, says "It's true, YES."
The wife of a lifetime, the children
of our capricious moments,
friends and neighbours, women,
men and beasts walking the street —
where do they turn towards
to confirm their sheer weight on me?

There're times when the overarching sky
shrinks into an invisible sight,
the sun and the moon pay back
their light to another world
in mysterious absence, and even
the stars withdraw into the wish
from which they sprouted long ago.

What slavish belief has kept
the nearer things together, palpable

like these lean fingers, defying
all possibilities of another presence?
The truth of things behind things,
in spite of things, because of things?
The old belief in everything to be where
they are, increasing in weight
through common night and day,
disregarding extraordinary absences,
night-time departures of the mind?

The Captive Hand

Today we shall talk of the small things.
Of how, yesterday, the hand failed to write
the line it had kept deferring
every time it wanted to write.
Of the new line, shadowed by
the ghosts of past words, teased by
their incandescence and pride.
Of how one small defeat can shatter
this brittle health of the heart and the mind.
Of the defeat that you had only spoken
to yourself about when, elsewhere,
the earthy and the strong had been
ransacking the gates of human speech.
Of the defeat about which no one knew;
it was your very own,
holding you in incredible captivity.
Could one never attempt to loosen
the destroying hold of time
on one's power to transmit
the things one owns?
Today we shall talk of the small things.
Of your steadily failing hold
on the modest words on your hands,
in your small hands.
Of how, yesterday, the hand failed to write.

Acquaintance with Fire

It arrived with the kind of simmering light
that we most often associate with
angelic places, with a halo
of ancestral radiance about its face,
the blinding sparkle of the midsummer
tropical sun about its eyes.

We knew that it was all going to be
different, that all our dark thoughts
and long, lurid phases of depression
were about to be taken care of
by luminescent hands, by lips that shone
with the warmth of the first sun.

It looked into our eyes (now seeing
nothing except the future) and smiled.
It knew we needed that too —
we had turned poor indeed.
The wishes had to be carefully
retrieved, set in order,
and renewed through a heat
that was gentle in its purpose,
the hopes renovated by temperate hands,
so that they retained those hands' warm wish
to preserve and sustain our human needs.

A year quietly went past while
every little thing around us watched
its fairy walk, the tiny feet
hardly touching the ground on which
they were supposed to walk.
Every little thing listened
to its talk, meant for none,
conveying, without our knowledge,
something that kept us together, bound
to its artless words that soon withdrew
into a zone of hushed smelting,
a shining area of mixture and absorption.

Our separate griefs came together
slowly, without even our least effort,
as though we never existed in ourselves
but elsewhere, under the watchful eye
of someone always caring, taking note of
every detail and yet perceiving
a common answer. Our tall claims
to supremacy, adulthood, our fugitive cheer —
all of these went into its melting pot,
and what it gave back was something
that we were seeing for the first time —
a shifting and radiant mass of dreams
that we merely touched and concluded.

Today, we wait for its childish pranks too —
of making a fire that we are yet to see,
of putting together vegetables, fruits, diapers
and written words into a utensil large enough
to hold such other things that we feign possessing,
giving us back what we always wanted:
the astral heat of the stars' light, the light
of an irretrievably-lost ancestral bliss.

Trees, Far and Near

Beyond the familiar roads, grinning
and rough with the load
of bullock-cart wheels,
and crisscrossing as if the town
were a puzzle to itself,
there's a tree with huge banyan branches
and spurious roots pushing back
to centuries. The river bank
doesn't seem to mind the quality
of the tree, the behaviour of its branches
attracting the farthest lives.
Each man who climbed up in the hope
that gravity's strange tricks
would return him to where he came
from, initially, has found himself fulfilled.
The cave's mineral darkness,
its extensive silences. That's where
one begins to rest at the end of whims
and failures of this life, away from the puzzle
that might hold others in loving company.

When the waters rise, the tree looks
different, sad indeed. Stranded
in the midst of defensive roles —
the ones that are so different
from what it has been used to.

The water rises by inches and feet until
one merely sees the softer branches
floating above the swirling river.
The tree appears too far away now
to tell us anything new;
one sits alone, reflecting on history.

And then, one turns to these
humbler trees around oneself, familiar
and near, and claiming little unless
someone thought they were our
ancestors' earth-bound souls
in green concealment. Thin as
air, quick to respond to
the slightest speech, each speaking
to its neighbours through a touch
so gentle that it almost goes
unnoticed, untouched. It seems
there's a lot of life still
around these trees, steaming above
every slight branch and leaf
and turning into the vapour
that our tired lungs exhale.
They accept our dispensable gift
of breath, wait and breathe,
gratefully give back what we seek.

Crossing Over

There're quite a few things to be crossed over
so that you may reach the farther shore.

The years that lie in wait, in the dark,
sprawling the river, ready to show themselves up

when you thought you were almost near
the place you wanted to reach, delaying

your journey with hopes of going back to
where you started, now darkened already.

And then the years that won't accompany you
despite your younger hopes of sustaining

yourself through the rites of passage,
cutting it short for a stay at a place

which you never wanted to see or know —
an island of paralysed haze, translucent air,

of unbelief fencing in your old pain in mid-river.
the possibility of others longing for your

companionship, the distracting cough
of your teenage child, your dear wife's

taking you over even before you knew
there was yet another, so close beside

you, starting to cross over
without much trouble, sooner.

The small call of the child who left
long before you, rising and falling

with the dark water's
changing behaviour, waiting

for someone to take it up
in his arms the same way

its father did, before it furtively
crossed over during one of the younger

nights in May of that year.
And then, your too human need

to postpone things, to defer
the crossing over until tomorrow

or the day after, the likelihood
of picking up the name floating

on the water in front of you,
acquiring something that you

always longed for, in spite of
yourself. The fear of drowning

in the water, the usual excuses
to keep yourself here longer than

your conscience wanted. The fascination
of waiting, the commitments of the future.

The Farther Shore

It takes a long time before
the eye reaches there.

A lone tree waiting, without
shadow or purpose;

a figure moving along its luminous borders,
undisturbed by what happens here.

The world ends there, and what
lies beyond is only what the mind

so competently conceives
during hours of pain and pleasure.

What distance lies between me
and that other shore except

the width of the river, now
dry, sand-bare, with only

an enlarged cover
of the sky and air

above its vast stretch of
luminescence and prolonged hour?

The mocking highland wind from the west
travels towards the Bay of Bengal

in the grim disguise of a dream lover.
The distant picture stays, the watch extends,

as my weak hands lean towards what could be
the very beginning of a long separation.

Dreaming Among Autumn Insects

Despite the small-time humming
of those seasonal insects,
the body shows itself everywhere —
under the tall sun, within
the dark that is believed to hold
the very last things.
Looking at the sky during a power failure
in the evening, in early summer,
and imagining the stars beyond
the stars, you think of the decision
you took so gracefully yesterday,
forgetting what lay ahead
of your waking dreams —
the small cut on the right forefinger
that wouldn't let you open the pen
in an easy, comfortable way,
time's smoky, unaccountable ways —
as if to dream today
were yet another means
of taking care of all the waiting days.

What if the harsh flesh
doesn't yield where it should,
thus giving the dreams their due —
in light, when strange-looking children
beg for your too human forgiveness;

in the dark, when your woman
speaks of the warmth that had been absent
ever since you started imagining
what other things the body could do
except sleep and wait.
The small things remain to be touched
in spite of the nightly games
of the mind's devising;
the celebrations of life aren't over yet.
What could the body do today, before
the memory of yesterday fades
with the crow's early, half-throated call,
or tomorrow, several years from now,
except sleep and wait?

The winged insects have been
innumerable and dead for a long time now,
and your pretentious body watches
the tiny red ants, numberless
and ready as ever, all over the floor,
busy with their food, simply,
without thoughts of tomorrow or yesterday.

They Have Been Telling Things

They've been telling things
for a long time now:
the gifts of history
and humble men that we
didn't know how to keep;
the embankments that
haven't been used properly;
the high northern mountains,
the felled trees, the dreams
shifted to the next century;
the air that we don't know
how to breathe.

Things that our
unthinking ears
tend to believe.
Unkind things, too harsh
for our frail and failing skins.
Things about things
that had lost themselves already
long before their time,
in the darker texts of our minds.

Home

Home is where we are, today,
this early morning hour. And we wish it
to remain as it is. With white eyes
staring at us from every corner,
thin legless bodies walking the corridor
at night, when we pretend to sleep.

There's always someone else
occupying the chair beside mine when
I begin to dine, with my children and wife.
There're always strange hands, waiting
to greet me when I return from outside,
graying fingers moving quietly over
handwritten pages and sketches, as if
to know and rectify my long-past errors.

There're times when we welcome strangers
as relations, as if the blood which flowed
in their veins gently spoke to our
matching blood in whispers, when we
stood or moved among others' company —
our bodies as pale and spectral as theirs,
eyes nearly lidless, unblinking, staring
into things of tomorrow, of next year, into
matters that'll end with our century.

Our wan hands take hold of things
that we know belong to others,
our lips utter sounds that do not
ever make an intelligible word
or phrase, but only a dark bluish mass
of matter that sprawls in the air
we breathe, urging us to watch
and listen to long-extinct sounds.

The things we think we possess
are owned by people we've only heard of
but never seen, although their good wishes
seem to be with us, for how else
could we possess what we didn't own?
At times a voice floats through
the humid midnight air, returning us
to our obligation to stay where we are.
Our home, perched among our
children's grudging smiles, hands
that are reluctant to take or give;
the dim, eventful faces from elsewhere
that could as well belong to the future
as they did to the passing and the past,
staying on in indefinite exile.

The Other Place

For Andrei Tarkovsky

1.

Since to be here is to be everywhere,
where was the need to go out to
a place that promised to be different?
Those who had left for it, earlier,
were either mad with themselves
or had had for long a true animal's
suicidal hunger. They never returned
to our quarters, and now they
need not, having gone out to witness
what was here already —
the grey-blue sea, swelling up
repeatedly to a shape that recalls
the day of Creation, the birth of
the child who knew all about us,
unerring extension of life, the resumption
of the wish to travel to an elsewhere place.

2.

The souls move in forms that are
familiar to this body —
the stolen, obsolete forms of yesterday,
more stoical though than their originals,
accepting without protest the heart's
temporary defeats, indifferent

to the possibility of a periodic restoration.
How small and ill even the soul looks
longing to achieve a body
that was never, never its own,
in the preposterous outlines of the body's details!
But we know, it longs for authentic company too;
it longs for this body that speaks
to its soul in tenuous whispers, as if
it didn't know how to speak, as if
a single touch could revive its surrogate human speech.
Which hitherto neglected remains of this body
do those distant souls pursue? This body
of yesterday, forgotten even by that which
until recently, so thoroughly knew
the undisclosed shadows within its too familiar blood?

3.

As for me, I'd rather stay here,
among thin trees thinning still,
lakes gradually drying up over the years,
pictures of snow and winter imported
from the north, with this body.
Although, looking up at the sky
during late evenings, I think of
the stars beyond the stars, of
the impossibility of every modest wish
that I'm supposed to cope with;
of far-seeming transactions that displace
the scrupulous allotments of the soul.
The "other place" is here, somewhere
between the soul and this wintering body
conspiring with the soul how to prolong
its own impatience with time and failure.

Something Else

Remembering Raymond Carver

There's always something else to these lines,
always someone behind you, watching.

You and the women and men who are elsewhere, sharing
our children's request to be near them, always.

The things that you use every day
without prior thought, the bed on which

every night you await your sleep,
your very own hours of the night,

your ill-timed sleep, desired rest of a lifetime —
there's always something else to these,

something other than ourselves
or objects we pretend to possess.

There're times when we feel something else
slowly coming to its fruition and flourish

through us, accomplishing its greenness
in the leaves' abandon, smiling

through the lean dead branches of an old
banyan tree, now waiting for its conclusion.

At the end of a period of defiant cheer, when
we lie exhausted, thinking what other line

might return us our plain human pride,
it hangs above us, smiling at our absences.

Who are we to think of others anyway,
or even ourselves, our children and friends,

our days and nights? It seems
all of them belong elsewhere, only

faintly nurturing that place's true character,
maturing into nothing beyond their own frail forms.

Something is always missing in the things
we use, the persons we care for —

something that teases us to believe
that we've come to the end of things

in its absence, amid its withdrawing ways.
Something which caused these lines,

pushed every word to a place that was
a lie long before it took its stanzaic place.

At this time, elsewhere, a lone sparrow
is calling out for someone who isn't

anywhere around, a slight voice speaking to
itself, consuming each moment of its mistaken time.

You know, it's always something else,
something other than the words in these lines.

Now

The bells toll almost all
over this small, ancient town;

street dogs howl through
the night and their ignorance;

crackers saved from
the last *Diwāli*

burst through the last few minutes
of the old year's damp winter air.

There's someone yet
lying quiet and old

somewhere, on the bed
of his own making,

curled up like a child
under a quilt, looking

for its mother
in the dark warmth

so cautiously gained
over a whole evening's

struggle with the ultimate
December pain and cold —

someone friendless, unowned,
without even the shadow of a year

attached to his name.

A Different Picture

You, who at this time last year
had walked through the nights,
your shoulders carrying your blind faith
in sleep's natural course, are now
struggling in bed for the unusual sleep,
the bones' undeserved rest.
You are not to blame of course.
Time has thrown a long, patient wait for things
all about the floor, now irrevocably full
with your children's mute toys, once-useful
building blocks of hope, minutes interlocked.

The game ends now, at the night's
suburban hour, within the heart's chambers
that open and close in their own obsolete manner.
No word or deed or prayers for mercy
can restart the game now.
What after all are words except old broken toys
of a past time that find their place more easily
elsewhere than this house of a wishful order?
What deed of hand, heart or mind can restore
your children's much-neglected desires?
The prayers have turned into a habit
of repeated sounds that spill, like your
own sleep, all over the clean floor.

There's little we can do now except
deferring the use of our own sleep,
recalling old prayers once more.
Night is its own answer
to our naive questions regarding
our nights to take care of ourselves.
Today, we merely wait for
bodiless words to consume us
by their ominous declaration:
You've had enough; you may not ask for more.

The Return of the Enemy

They are back again, with their
surrogate tongues, on these wide open
corridors of pain, wearing archaic masks
on which a needle-thin smile sits unerringly.

The hurt is somewhere here, around
those clean words, polished to a glorious shine.
On mornings such as this one, when
our children look for us everywhere,
including all those places where
our bodies are supposed to be,
they cast their own nets of words.
We hear, but do not believe in what they are.

Belief is where a touch
as old and loving as our years
hovers between skin and skin, searching
for itself, unaware that yet somewhere,
at some dark point of time, it was
disowned by everyone except us.

Dear child: I know how a hurt
quietly possesses you, makes you
a part of us, despite
our best efforts to leave you alone.
I know, you never came here

to learn our subtle twists of phrase
or know one smile from another.

They're back with us.
And hence, let us at least be together
this day, this staying minute of today.
May they use their speech where
no one listens, may their words
move back to wherever they came from.
Dear child: the once-disowned, lonely touch
is here still, drifting between us,
looking for our waiting skin to take it in.

Giving Away

For fourteen years I've been speaking
to myself, in the dark, enclosed by
the tall walls of this room,
shutting the lights off its eight windows.

Can you ever believe it, you who
shine in your talk's phosphorescent light,
walk the streets where you slowly,
unquestionably turn those
unsuspecting ones into good listeners?
You wouldn't know what it means
to speak all alone to oneself
for this long a time, all alone,
when the spirit comes in and goes,
nonchalantly, looks betrayed somehow.

I know, somewhere I have to stop speaking
to myself, now that even my
twenty-month-old child has started
suspecting my lips and speech,
my ability to give and take.
This, my room, is full already
with unexpected speech, the air dark
with a shy, obscure breath.

Even if I wanted to, how could I move?
I have to carry this room out now

when others — fine givers —
have shown their refusal to talk?
But the spirit now waits
in a forgiving gesture, sparing its time
to witness the final moving out,
choosing to stay on
longer than ever for the final act.
There is no time to lose.

Drumbeats in the Afternoon

The beating could be heard across the town's
dividing lanes, emerging from the end,
spreading over the afternoon, quietly taking over
the warm winter on the coast.

A beat of something leaving, arriving
at a regular pace at our mind's
imagining, increasing in number
as we begin to count their probable numbers.

As clear as the sound of footfalls
approaching our waiting ears
within a dream of departures, falling
to the rhythm of ancient faces disappearing.

Harsh as broken sleep, lonely as that sleep's
precisely counted minutes in reverse,
floating back to the beginning of history
in the midst of our numbness, dumb wonder.

Who has left the afternoon so far behind?
What kind of going has left us so solely to ourselves?
The recently released dreams of the old? The faith of a woman
taking advantage of her man's lingering years?

Our sleeping children wait for the afternoon to flower
inside their competing pictures of the future,

unaware of how the February sun now shines
over an incomplete picture of our own making.

Different sounds prevail now, lonelier notes
of a lifetime of forgetting, a remembrance
of losing things, an afternoon left far behind
by the past drumbeats of another land, another kind.

Yet Another Year

Another year is lost. Another looking forward
in the hope that all roads would lead to the desired
place. Another face, which had almost found itself
as if for the first time in its own place.

Only the increasing winter has stayed
through a quiet change in dates. A winter
more harsh than remembering the nearest things,
more sure of itself than every kind of foretelling

I've waited for yet other things to sail into
the frozen cavities of the mind — the morning noises
of children perspiring in spite of the continuing cold
even as grandmothers pray for their own departing.